Frangipani

Joe Pascoe

First published 2020 by Reading Sideways Press
20 Tennyson Street, Richmond, VIC, 3121

readingsidewayspress.com
readingsidewayspress@gmail.com

Copyright @ Joe Pascoe 2020

My very special gratitude goes to Andy Fuller and Nuraini Juliastuti.
The encouragement of Adam Bos from the NDIS is also acknowledged.
Very special thanks to Brigitta Isabella for a beguiling and brilliant foreword.

Cowrie shell watercolour by Sam Golding
Collages by Joe Pascoe

Designed by New Pessimism Studio (Yogyakarta, Indonesia)

ISBN 978-0-6482610-8-7

For Robert Nelson, an art historian
with a spectacular mind

Waves

The waves they came in
They showed me a shell
The waves came in
And made me feel well.

CONTENTS

Waves	7
Foreword: Frangipani: a tent made from poems and collages *Brigitta Isabella*	13
Part 1: Threading pearls	21
Sunny frangipani	23
Painting a beach	24
Sand castles	26
Inverloch beach	28
Clouds	29
River swim	32
Bend in the river	33
Angel	35
Part 2: Chipped marbles	37
Things that interest children	38
Boyhood weapons	40
The Coca Cola Yo Yo	41
Comics	43
Mars	44
Fish & Chips	46
Ode to chocolate	47
Fish tank	48
$2 Shop	48
The mystery of the socks	50
Ear plugs	51

Part 3: At work 53

Petrol station	54
Train driver	55
Thank you	56
Kind spirits	57
Shop girl	58
Telemarketers' dinner party	59
Mirror	61
Meeting	62
BCC	63
Hole punch	64
Tuesday's clothes	65
Emperor penguins	68
Photographer	69
Tent	70
The good accountant	71

Part 4: Believing 73

Peace be with you	74
Buddhist student	75
Word shape	76
You Yangs in the night	78
Two Nuns	82
Evening meal	84
Curly haired cyclist	85
Burnt butterfly	87
The magician	88
Secrets	89
Natasha Tontey	90
Octopus	91
Beautiful wharf	93
Spell	95

Angels in the playground	96
In flower	98
Satan	99
Warship	101
Must	103
Re-enactment	104
Waterlilies	105

Part 5: Things in my pockets — 107

Lions	108
Silhouetted by life's riddle	109
Cowboy	111
Goodnight campfire	113
Droplets	115
Fairies	116
Poison	117
Old swimming pool	120
High in the hot stand 3XY Top 40	124
Library foyer	125
Mountain	128
Wind torn pages	130
About Joe Pascoe	133
About Reading Sideways Press	134

FRANGIPANI: A TENT MADE FROM POEMS AND COLLAGES

What's going on inside your mind while queuing at a petrol station? While sitting on a train seat on your way to work, or while standing in a minimarket checkout line?

In these transit moments, during the time when bodies are immobile due to the act of waiting necessitated by rituals of urban daily life, Joe Pascoe seems to be mobilizing his mind to look for poetry. At least that's what I imagine—having never met Pascoe in person—after reading *Frangipani*. As a reader, I believe that besides speculating on meanings that may flourish from a certain text, it is also fulfilling to wonder why an author would endure the inevitable solitude of writing poetry.

I found one possible answer to such a question from my encounter with Pascoe's recent collection of poems. Here is one of Joe's

poems, one of my favorites from the book,
titled "Petrol Station", quoted in full length:

> Ok we are here
> Smoothly in place
> Alongside
> Carefully
> Simple enough
> Walk across
> Diagonal and quick
> Past the lollies
> Line up straight
> Like the cars
> No bumps
> Keep it neat
> Tight and pro
> In what we both do
> Out the door
> On alert
> Click belts
> Nudging away
> From the petrol station.

The poem holds a quotidian scene of a petrol station, an easily ignored scene for its anticipated status as a non-event. There's no fire, fight, or accident that could make news. The poem does not try to brand it to be more phenomenal or eventful either. What it does is expose the sequential seams of a routine, things that go "simply enough" but "carefully"—to borrow Pascoe's words from the poem. Pascoe's insistence on giving assiduous attention to details is a work of undoing established relations between words and objects. What has been marked as familiar gets another chance to be re-marked in the realm of linguistic play.

Perhaps then, the act of writing poetry can be a soft, yet stubborn resistance against simplifications or what has been taken for granted as "simple"— things that should not be thought of further.

In a time where being always busy doing something is often normalized as the good and productive work ethos, Pascoe's poetic labor is an appeal to be "unproductive". To sit and write a poem is to exercise the endurance of one's consciousness towards the "simple", "irrelevant" and "unnecessary" things. Such consciousness is appealing, and somehow contagious. Beyond the book and without his poems before me, I continue to see poetry in petrol stations and other places or scenes that I encounter every day.

What appears monotonous or automatic-mechanical in the rhythm of everyday life is disrupted when the uneventful image of reality is reconfigured through word play. In many of Pascoe's poems, like the "Petrol Station", it gestures towards a motion that follows the stream of time passing by. The motion of Pascoe's poems does not work by representing a movement, but rather by demonstrating it. It feels like you're on a ride with the poet. The poem itself is on the move: "Poems on trains/ Going for a ride/ Moving as I write them/ Rolling along on steel rails/ That's their rhythm (From "Bends in the River").

At the same time, like all works of art, the act of poetry writing willfully tries to make things last beyond the present moment. Writing a poem is also making a shelter for ephemeral matter. The fast and steady linear movement from origin A to destination B is slowed down as we take a stopover and wander in the shelter of poetry.

What happens during the slowing down process is an expansion of the qualitative duration of consciousness. In many instances of Pascoe's poems, the shelter of poetic language offers unexpected wisdom from a locus of singularities that can be found throughout the homogenized regulars. Such unexpected wisdom floats from his poems that zooms in through ordinary objects such as socks, earplugs, a fish tank, a yoyo, and even the purple pack of Cadbury chocolate.

Pascoe articulates these objects by their singularities, but not as exceptions to the commonplace. The commonplace or the ordinary are not appreciated their submission or difference to their established definition. It is rather characterized by the difference of each moment it is being thought of or carefully appraised by Pascoe's poetic labor. His poems push the threshold of what is recognizable in an ordinary object or in everyday scenery. A case in point: a pair of socks is never simply a pair of socks anymore, for its materiality has been enhanced and recaptured by Joe's admirable repertoire of words. "Rough or wobbly/ Warm and woolly / White cotton / There is something they do / To deceive you" ("The Mystery of the Socks")

Pascoe's poems are channeling knowledge discourses that are not about gaining comprehensive understanding of reality under the scientific eye of a magnifying glass. Zooming in is a gesture for tweaking the density of an object, thus what is at stake is less a matter of epistemological than dramatic. Knowing is much richer than gaining a fixed certainty of an object when it allows awareness of one's feelings and imagination to involve in the complex structure of understanding. In regards to the dramatology of the everyday life, one might suggest that certain subjects, such as the panorama of a beach for example, have often been exhausted by the cliché performance of poetic language. The tranquil imageries of white sand, champagne sunset, or cascades of blue waves have been massively reproduced in tourist advertising. As if leaving no room for novel experience because everything has been harnessed to stereotypical leisure images–products.

A handful of Pascoe's poems stir his recreational experiences on the beach against the stultified realm of the cliché. Through the craft of poetry making, he tries to personalize the common landscape into his own authentic belongings, showing the pleasure of rediscovering and repainting the mundane image of a beach—in his words—"to surprise the eye" ("Painting a Beach"). The element of surprise can also be found in Pascoe's careful observation through the laws of his own sensory perspective upon, to name a few, the erotic texture of octopus tentacles or the magical spell of a tiger cowrie stranded on the beach. The strongest lesson that I learned from reading *Frangipani* is less about what Pascoe observes than about how he observes. To write a poem with Joe's method is to exercise our curiosities and to seek for the delicate surprises in the grains of everyday life.

As art historian Robert Nelson stated in the foreword to Pascoe's first book, *Gum Tree Burning* (Reading Sideways Press, 2019), Pascoe's professional experience as a curator and museum director has trained "his readiness to think in images" (p.19). To add a supplementary interpretation to what Nelson says, I would like to suggest that Pascoe's act of poetry writing is also embodying the gesture of visual artistic production. What I want to bring into discussion is Pascoe's collages that accompany the poems in both the former as well as his latest books. Co-existing is perhaps a better word than accompanying, as in my view Pascoe's collages can be put in a dialogue with his poems.

The intertwining relationship between the artistic modes of collage and poetry is clearly articulated in one of Joe's lines: "Collage out of a poem / Poem out of a collage / There is something in between / Unseen" ("Word Shape"). In the ambiguous space of "something in between" the creative power of reconfiguring words and shapes, both in Pascoe's craft of collage and poetry, embraces chance, incident, and improvisation. Collage as an artistic mode has a distinctive place in the histories of art, and such broad topic would not be rehearsed here. Manual "cut and paste" shall serve as a plain explanation to the process of making collage. Joe's collages, however, are the result of ripping or tearing, rather than cutting. Ripping a paper will reveal its tiny fibers, inner color and textured edges, which are not evident when a paper is slickly cut with scissors. I'd like to think the way Pascoe breaks down an object in his poems is tearing out the flatness of the ordinary. It is from the raw and tactile edges of the torn ordinary where Pascoe's poems emerge.

It is now left to the reader to zoom in and out

to Pascoe's collages and poems. To configure and reconfigure their delicacy. As for me, who is privileged to be one the first readers of this book, I see flower petals in the collages next to the content list page. The more I look at them, I see wild bushes, untamed flames, a light feather… The list should go on as far as our imagination continue to serves us. Pascoe's poems, as I mentioned earlier, assemble a shelter to keep the ephemerals. The structure of the shelter that he builds is not a huge and sturdy edifice. It is a tent. A bit fragile, but still offers some warmth. The tent is secured with tent pegs made of "A mixture of premise / And promise / And time" ("Tent"). I imagine the tent fabric is made from colorful collages sewn together. Come inside, the poet will show us what he has in his pocket: the slippery pearls and the chipped marbles. There are infinite stories that we can hear if we allow ourselves to dwell a bit longer inside the tent.

Brigitta Isabella is a researcher based in Yogyakarta, Indonesia. Her research trajectory revolves around the geo-poetical aspect of mobility and migration. She is one of the members of Kunci Study Forum & Collective.

PART 1:
THREADING PEARLS

JOE PASCOE

Sunny Frangipani
for Trevor and Michele Fuller

Let me dream
In the sunshine
Let's live
In perfumed wonder

Yellow and white
Flowers spinning round and around
Dizzy in the noon heat
Silently shimmering in the night.

Walk by with eyes open
Every step a simple faith
As it should be
Pearly petals in fives
With strong yellow dots
And thick green leaves in ribbed fans
Lush sprays smiling
It's so easy the way the branches turn out

The roots nourished by messy droppings
Holding moisture and hope
And now covered by evening's cape
As I brush my way home.

The muses stayed at the river and learned to hunt
They parlayed with their spiritual
brethren in the bush
And tried to be there for them
It was to become a very long dance
Continuing on today
For all who wish to see.

Painting a Beach

for Fiona Murphy and Craig O'Neil

Needing blue
In these words
and in the air
I'm sitting in the sky
Floating in the
words I write

Loosely
Letting things darken
And move to moave
I rest

                                      Looking up
                                      Off the hillside
                                      Chipped waves are
                                      cupping the light
                                      Washing darker notes
                                      against the cliffs

The beach is yellow
So they say
Though it would need
A Naples yellow
and light-grey
Stretched out thin,
and touched by brown
To surprise the eye
Like a rock can do

                          We are dry
                          Walking along a
                          drunken edge
                          Taking steps
                          in less time
                          Then the beating
                          of the waves
                          Stepping over sheets
                          of beery foam
                          Our mouths
                          marry into one
                          On this nameless shore
                          Of white paper
                          On which I draw

                          Two dots
                          Merging almost
                          into one
                          As we fall in love
                          Endlessly again.

Sand castles

for Bob, Eve and John Pascoe

On the beach
In the beach
Legs twisted to one side
Tummy tight to the right

Packing sand into the red bucket
A bit sun worn
Turn over and pat down
And make another

Incise a moat
Scrape it with my blue spade
The wave comes in with glee
It fills the channel and surrounds my castles

I decide on a wall too
Choking the sand in small hands
Adult monsters walk by
Part of the landscape which is mine
Smack it down
And firmly patted into shape
Elaborate now
A British sea town
On an Australian beach

There are solid walls all around
A careful gap to fool the wave
It fills my moat
From the sea comes another beautiful wave
Challenging all
My structure survives, pretty well

I leave it alone
   Knees under my chin
      And watch it soften the fort,
      in the foam,
      as the tide decides
      to come in
    It is time for a swim.

Inverloch beach

Walking up to the driftwood bonfire stacks
On Inverloch beach
Straggly open tepees
Promising paganism
Could be for the winter solstice I wonder
Tidying up the sand
strewn with large driftwood.

Not really like a storm
More of a landscape
Trees turned and twisted
Sucked by the tides
Pushed by the onshore winds
Over the cold ocean seas
Strangely without a language
A calligraphy of sorts
The words of the wind
Written on the sand
Which none of us can understand.

Clouds

Diving the clouds
Flying through
Our small plane
Noisy in the quiet
Our motors chopping
and beating
Droning with less speed
In the cockpit
Confusing dials yet
right on course

We drop
Almost in plonks
Bumping down like
a billy cart
Settling on the ground
Refuelling in a
country paddock
Somehow feeling safe
'Cos I've seen it all work

Staring down at the ground
Leaves now in focus
The ground changes
in colour
As we wrestle in with the air
Down easily, gliding
onto another tarmac

Taking off
Tanks full
Full throttle, drawn back
Full sound

Full revs
Lifting
We lean forward
Urging flight
Relax in the sky
Open a jar
Artichoke hearts eaten high
Tasty and prescient

A heart can pickle
And taste strange
Many years later
When kept in a glass jar,
screwed tight

Clouds stay in my mind
Gliding and turning
Through the soft clouds
Smiling to each other
in god's hands
We were happy then
Together on an adventure

We crash landed
Some years later
You were disappointed
And I can see that now
As the door closed
Behind you

I went inside
Inside myself that is
Locked away and rusting
Until ...
Flaking away
The sky spoke again

A ragged dagger
showed me the way
Amazing!
Zeus' arm in the sky
White and red-gold
Cracking through
An odd thing,
jiggered and real
Revealed, promised, given
I flew anew.

River swim

We swam chopping about
Pausing to smooth the river's skin
Bodies covered in the brown water
Encased in this bend in the Goulburn
A sandy beach backing to the car park
Tough logs, tough kids, black footy shorts
Swinging from a tatty rope
Tarzan with tatts seeks Jane
We got out
Dripping off
Like champagne settling
Everybody equal in this country town.

So many years ago
Always feeling fragile
Just flesh softened by air
Trying not to stare
Stay a while she said
I wish I had I guess
But thinking no
Too far to go
Where was home then?
Only in my moving car
Going somewhere
I couldn't care
I was broken back then.

Bends in the river

Start close in
 But I'm closed in by too much clutter
  In my life
   In my room
    History's tokens take up space
     Can you pack it away?
      Or place them in storage
       Mash them into poems
        As a first step

         Opening a door to feelings
          See how it slides
           Poems on trains
            Going for a ride
             Moving as I write them
              Rolling along on steel rails
               That's their rhythm

                I could tell you where they done
                 Which stations, when
                  As the doors slide open
                   Somewhere along the long line
                    People get on
                     People get off
                      I count them, sort of
                       They hop inside my sentences

                        I used to direct an art gallery
                         But the countryside
                          was not bucolic
                           It was hard and hot
                            With a ceramic
                             collection to match

Which melted my heart
 As I bought and bought
  And the people smiled again.

   It's true, all of it
   Into love I fell
    Furnace and fire
     Smashed me to pieces
      To reform as a kinder man
       In time

        Rewards they come and go
         There was something else there though
         The style and pace of Shepparton,
         washes over me, even now
         It had a start and an end
         That river with its bend.

Angel

for Lyndel Wischer

Angel
Sun shone on
Carefully captured
Our gold rings.

JOE PASCOE

PART 2:
CHIPPED MARBLES

Things that interest children

Dog years
Cat years
Hours in a day on other planets
Days in a year on Mars
How many yards in a mile
Miles per hour
Pennies and cents
How six can equal five
How to tell a lie
Train stop names in order
Routes on Sundays to special places
Handkerchief, as a word

      And screens

Quite a lot,
and today it's much more
Latest things
What's cool, what's new?
And, and, and again
A world pumped tight
Ready to explode

Sone kids like systems
Some want to be in a team
Some fall short
And despise themselves
Others turn into mini adults
But still long for a dog

They still need your attention,
your love,
be a diamond,
a permanent jewel,
for *them*.

Boyhood weapons

A small dart
Made from a pin, fuse wire, a
matchstick and paper fins
Paper water bomb
Rubber band stretch along a ruler
Two rubber bands, looped to form a slingshot
To fire bent nails

Spit

Wet tennis ball, flung hard
Ouch!
Back of the leg, red mark,
no mercy, when fleeing

Flicked towel in the swimming pool lockers,
Tiny bit homo you homo
Thumb tacks on a seat
Never did it

Oh yes,
Ganging-up
Teasing, focus on a detail

Sticks and stones may break your bones
But WORDS?
Best and worst of all
... words ...
They hurt, cry boy.

JOE PASCOE

The Coca Cola Yo Yo

Yo yo
Up and down
Soft string wound around
Beautiful symmetry spinning free

Flick and hold
Walk on the floor
Twitch again and watch it climb

Alive in the hand
Vibrations running thru
Balance in the mind
A meditation
Bending time

Open to adventure
Swaying and rocking
Climbing again
Outwards
Around the world

Do it once
Do it twice
Thrice!
Getting good now

Slow to a stop
Check the string
Wrap it firm
Tuck it in
Smooth in the pocket

Nicely done.

Comics

Comics
Phantom hunts again
Emerging dark from the pages
To enter my life
Saving people
Loving his animals
Going on into cities
From the jungle
This family man
King of the pigmies
Sure fire shot

        Super man
        Batman
        They had the lot
        Impossible quests
        Just in time
        Each action in a box
        Hard, adhesive
        Andy Warhol?
        Piss weak

                Incredible Hulk
                Spidey and the Joker
                Eccentric and colourful
                Beyond didactic
                I feel it in the brain
                Fragments of furry
                Plots twisted into knots
                Knots cut
                Falling, falling,
                caught inches from
                the pavement

Mars

On Mars
At a guess
New to me
Twitching in the suit
Helmet like a bubble
Pure egg form
Clear all around
Protecting me
Suit hisses a little
Valves easing and pressing
Gloves stretching
Finely embracing my fingers

Two-year flight
Semi dead
Breathing slow
Drugged in day long shifts
Blowing time away
No pain or drain
Waking now
Forward looking
Calming the self
Away from the ship

Spaceman
Most alone
Alone you do not kill
Just provide data
And live on

One year
Two
Move through
Contribute to humankind

Mind controlled for a while
Decay and terror
Or
Terror and then decay
Drugs in my mind
Giving me moods

Stunning Mars
Very amazing up close
Wish for nothing more
My secret.

Fish & Chips

Staple of the seaside economy
Key to my heart
Expertly judged
Understood by many

Price and flavour
Handed over with due care
Salt and lemon
Condiments that add flair

Sometimes the fish
Sometimes the chips
Come together just right
Perfectly packaged in white

Once a Friday night delight
Grilled or fried
Flake
Is all right

Chips chips chips
It's mainly about the salt
Piles of potato
Can make you feel pretty tight

I could give you hints
On where to go
I vouch for Williamstown Beach
You know

Solo or in company
Summer or winter
Seagulls none or plenty
Its fish & chips for me.

Ode to Chocolate

for Solomon Nelson

A love you can eat
Savour as it melts
And lightly chew
Roll and swirl into a glue
Feel it
Within you

I prefer Cadbury
An ancient firm
Pleasant and defining
Suggest chilled and in moderation
Let it rest sweetly and linger
No need to swamp the palette
Small particles ride the taste buds
Ducking out between teeth
Bandits in a gunfight
Kapow!
Visit the wildest aisle
The purple pack.

Fish tank

Live nightmares
Wriggling in a tank
Guaranteed to die
Dying alive
Before my eyes

As I fish
For a while
With less and
no feeling
Turning into colours
Grey and something
I cannot tell

They swim in
one direction
In the tiny tank
At an angled
pursing distance
Or just skidding
that way

Until
Bought
Cooked
Over.

$2 shop

Walking the aisles
So much to see
And feel and touch
And wonder at

Little creatures
Concepts at play
I do love the chances
Curating crazy circuses
With small change

Better than op shops
Somehow joyous
Symbols not smells
Kinetic and colourful
Closely compacted

Asian things
Amazing and
clear as day
Worlds next to each other
A thousand of them

Lucky two-dollar coin
Lucky adventures
everywhere
Buy some magic
100 spells
Glue them all together
Wake up in the morning
O what did I do?!

JOE PASCOE

FRANGIPANI

The mystery of the socks

for Olympia Nelson

I'm sure other people have
written this poem
A poem about socks
How they arrive in pairs
And leave in ones
Somehow escaping
Between the washing machine
And the line
Like POWs camouflaged
in the night
Somehow they take flight

They change lengths too
Turn black to blue
Rough or wobbly
Warm and woolly
White cotton
There is something they do
To deceive you

Whatever your strategy
They will keep ahead of you
Which after all
Is what they are meant to do.

Ear plugs

I've got my
ear plugs in

They're not
connected to
my phone

I've got my
ear plugs in

They help me
feel alone.

JOE PASCOE

*PART 3:
TO WORK*

Petrol station

Ok we are here
Smoothly in place
Alongside
Carefully
Simple enough
Walk across
Diagonal and quick
Past the lollies
Line up straight
Like the cars
No bumps
Keep it neat
Tight and pro
In what we both do
Out the door
On alert
Click belts
Nudging away
From the petrol station.

Train driver

Eye of a silver machine
With a long, twisting, hissing tail
Slithering on steel
Hissss!

Opens and closes
Scales breathing
On and off
Sometimes many sometime few
Sometimes furious
Other times slow

Passing each other
Crossing steel paths
Bells ringing
Level and smooth
Talking too
On its way

Long journeys
Connecting names and places
Hot or cold
Day and night
From home to work
And back again
A fine creature
This marvellous machine.

Thank you

String tugged tight
Just a finger flex
Drawing the paper taught
Brown glossy texture
Circa 1969
A parcel handed over
Plump with grey material
Measured with a flourish
Bolt unravelling with lumpy ease
Two metre chalk mark
Sliced with beautiful heavy scissors
Sharp and precise
A fine action
A magical skill

Material folded and refolded
Paper rolled out and screeched off
Brass cutter
Left on the sales bench
All assembled
Paper, string and fabric
Perfectly proportioned
Handed over
With a smile
With two hands
Sharing pride
Thank you.

Kind spirits

Aboriginal art
Helps the healing
In hospitals
It's the love
The purple and pinks
Simple non framing
Creating ease
Soaking the emotions
Of the diseased.

White walls and equipment
Data ticking over
Dots in the paintings
Data spots
Measuring every heartbeat
Counting down
With care and grace.

Shop girl

How are you?
Beep
Beep
Beep beep
Beep
I look at their goods
It matched them
Birthday party
Family meal
Pasta milk cheese
Salami figs on it goes
Bread bananas basics

Down the aisles
Looking to the music
Beep
Beep bop
Beeep
Bop bop
Cash out?

Eye contact.

Telemarketers' dinner party

Hi, I'm Colleen
Have you tried the bread?
It's 15 percent better
Or this dip could be yours
Thank you, Colleen
I was hoping to check these nuts
Are they in the package?
They could be Mandy
I can add them into the plan
on a monthly basis
But try them
Snap

Have you met George?
Strange crackle to the left
I'm George
We have some fine wine on special
Home delivered once a month
Reds and whites
Thank you George a glass please

Wrapped or open?
Open please and just one
Terrific party nice furniture
How is your mortgage?
Are these low-voltage and long lasting?
This conversation may be recorded
for training purposes
Let me switch you through

Now for main course
Fresh vegetables once a week
How nice no need to shop
Easy and light
Just use these sachets for flavour

Hi Colleen, doing well?
It's always good
Let me introduce you to Mary
She's from somewhere
How can I help you?
Could you do a survey?
It's about sex
On a scale of one to five
One being no thanks
Yes being fantastic
Would you like to do it again?
Look at the time
In other countries
Must make some calls
Love ringing people all day

That moment of weak hesitation
In like Flynn
Coffee anyone and dessert?
Some peaches and chocolate sauce
From your local supplier
It's been great
Thank you is there anything else today?
No thanks go away I feel soiled
Have a nice day
Odd pop.

Mirror

Mirror mirror
On the wall
Who is getting
The best haircut of all?

Words, glass, hair
and laughter
Fill the space
She snips
I feel
We chat
Of life

Where did you
have lunch
Suggesting adventures
Which flatter me
I reveal
She listened
A fond empathy
We probably all
say the same
Where we live
Our children
Quiet about our wives
The weight we carry
Lightened by the haircut
Restoring self confidence
With skill and style
An emotional groove
Happily occupied

Snip, comb, brush
Even
Product?
Gel and a poof of puff
Combed again
Real care
A close compassion
Without judgment
Helping me meet
the world
With more love.

Meeting

Office worker
You know what to do
You know the dates
And the rules too

You meet them in the foyer
It's a polite thing
Press the button
Lift opens
You do it again
Really so easily
It's your cage
They huddle in
Bags pressed
Then to the room to begin

You have no files
You have some weak smiles
Lay it out
Listen too
Making sure
They don't snare you

Meeting over
No notes taken
A clear indication
Of your satisfaction
Down down the lift
The ground floor feels heavy
For them.

BCC

I can tell you
But I can't tell him
That I told you

We whisper sideways
Pretending they did not see
Me telling you

I told you a lie
In strict confidence
To keep it true

You did not tell me
But I knew
Before you didn't say

I told myself
Something I knew was wrong
But needed to.

Hole punch

Two neat holes
Satisfying process
In advance of order
To paraphrase Marcel Duchamp
'In advance of the Broken Arm'
Paired with an excellent
pencil sharpener
The type affixed to a desk
A pen and folders to rule the world
Your own world
Sub divided
Drop files
The project defined by dates
And so on
Agenda, attachments
Tabled papers, et cetera, NB
From pay day to pay day
Swinging like Tarzan
Through the office politics.

Tuesday's clothes

Clean and black
For this is Melbourne
Where many seasons prevail
Swirling around our styles
Blending them in to one

Office workers in step
Forward to work
Already in their cubicles
At their monitors with a 20cms stare
Hello to their friends
Composed and ready
Log in with care

Through the streets
In coats and jumpers
Textures and earphone wires
Murmuring in their brains
A day to remember
Or not

Minor clothing oddities
Here and there
A football beanie and puffer jacket
In loyalty and faith
Though not corporate wear

Quietly building their lives
Nice people
Polite people
Often a little bit plump
With a fixed stare
And mild stomp

I like them
Drinking my coffee and sticky escargot
Enjoying my lot
Their sense of who they are
Framed by Flinders Street Station
This simple Tuesday morning
Devoid of any real despair

A city ticking over
Under its clocks
Tuesdays are fine
You are getting work done
You might have a list or diary
As the Monday meeting is already done

Settle back and work it out
As payday is coming about
Your clothes today need not be sharp
More in line with camouflage
So, stay safe and secure
And keep your spot.

Emperor penguins

Emperor penguins
Turning together
Huddled in coats and neatly groomed

Platform comes in
We shuffle slightly forward
Mourning not murmuring
As the train settles

Tall ones
Fat ones
Happy and sad
Yellow creased and black and white

Kind in a group
Determined by nature
Protecting our eggs

Off the nest
Gathering food from afar
A keen eye
Searching for partners

Warm on the inside
Cold outside
A subdued cacophony
Celebrating this Melbourne Tuesday
A quiet hooray!

Photographer
for John O'Neil

Sensitive as film
Tall as a tripod
Angled and fixed
People have no idea
How sensitive you are

Your truth
Your lens
Your eye
See the lie

The lie of the land
The lie of the moment
Click.

Tent

One letter
I can see one letter
At a time
You form somewhere
In my mind
In a word
A simple word
Linked to a thought
Wrapped in an emotion
To form a short line
Within a poem
Itself
A mixture of premise
And promise
And time
Secured like a single tent peg
To raise a tent
To raise a poem
Into which we may go.

The good accountant

They come
to me

Every year

I hear their
sins.

PART 4:
BELIEVING

Peace be with you

Holding New Zealanders together
So simply, so open
Strong, beautiful, real
Adorned in a Maori cloak
Bird colours and textures
Formed from history
Gracefully swaying, face ashine
This young mother of a nation
History and future together
Meaning and words together
Message of hope
In the same boat
Gliding on
Winds all around
Standing still in the centre
Those eyes that see
And receive
A leader from the heart
A heart made from her home
Her spirit, our spirit
Touch
Us, the earth and the sky
Peace be with you.

Buddhist student

Buddha
I did not look for you
I looked for Buddhism
Your first lesson

LaTrobe University
at night
Hand to the bookshelf
Looking for suffering
The four-part truth
It's circular logic
Absorbed as a truth
Held indifferently
By me
Art history student
Wary of stone gods
Yet happy with the text
As typed
As held
Re-read and re-
read for clues
Suffering is caused
by desire
Desire causes suffering
It seemed
That seemed true
Not great in itself
Too modest

Perhaps

The eight-fold path
Moderation in
all things
More modesty
More to say
More to live through
Where was nirvana
Found without desire
Sought without self
Harmless to all
A mantra

It helped.

Word shape

Spooked
It held so much meaning
Sand play
Laying it out
Turning it around
A life seen in perspective

And the intuitive selections
What magic
Tarot and luck
Why did it happen so
We are the same
With our loves
It seems

Collage
Ripping
Not ripped enough
Wild like bushes
I make a collage
Campfire becomes its name
Whilst tearing and remembering
Colored paper flames
Floating feelings
Overthinking
A recipe for stuckness

Too small
Fuss
Accidental elements
Take the hint
A lot of joy in collages
I whistle when I am joyful
That's true, that's true
Stopping before it stops

Collage out of a poem
Poem out of a collage
There is something in between
Unseen.

You Yangs

for Anthony Pearse

I went into the shadows
Following the soft path
Silken in the moonlight
Barely brushing by
Lingering only
To breathe evenly
With little effort
Glancing upwards at the rocks
Looking down to avoid
Any stubbing of feet
Feeling sideways at times
Arm half outstretched
Fingers curled but feeling
Almost bat like
Feeling the direction
Upwards and around
Slowly to a stop
Easy now
Resuming again
A bit impatient
Shortening of breath
Having to use my muscles
As the climb steepened
Swallowing air
Rising boredom and stress
As calculations flowed
Horizons cheating me
As the hill continued on
Alone it felt useless
But together it felt a challenge
As we measured ourselves
Against each other
Sharing the mountain

JOE PASCOE

A short pitch forward
Where the path opened
To a tough top
Occupying much bald space
Where there were only large boulders
Impervious to decay
In colours of grey
With scrabbly stones underneath
And straggly skinny plants
We looked at the composition
Defined a fine line
To ascend hands and knees bent
Avoiding false turns
Tight squeezes creating risk
Rising up at the imperial crest

The valley below
Laid out as smooth as a bedsheet
All asleep beneath the stars
Harmless and perennial in its desire
Not conquered by us
Only seen
Our gaze meant nothing
Mild perspiration was the reward
Which way to look?
The view tended to be framed to the east
With some north open and south
being the way we had come
Only west was barred
I can't remember why
Perhaps it had disappeared with the low sun
Withdrawing away

Sitting it became obvious
Time to return

Legs stiffening
The body thinking sleep was best
Eucalyptus scent releasing
Maybe insects flying
Hunters of the night
We slid off
Touched the dirt
Tried to make sure
Edged toward the way
Looking unlikely in reverse
And time was different
Quicker in its bat
Moving down exercised our calves rather than thighs
Toes instead of ankles
More or less
Remembering to stand straight
Not crouched
Arms just away from the body
Forming wings in semi flight
Stepping sideways skidding about
Speeding up out of sight

Soon at the car park
Over to the pine trees
Heap up the fine needles
A soft lie
Warm too
The wind blew
Comfortable and nearly asleep
Secure and safe
Knowing the You Yangs
That little bit more.

Two Nuns

Sunlight on the tall stone building
Laughing nuns touch on the arm
How cute, a red beard! Irish accent, is he new?
Don't know, she said
Disinterestedly
Let's have tea

I've been here for twenty years
My shoes are wearing out
I don't feel any closer
I still have the same doubts

She wonders aloud
Pauses her biscuit
Her friend feels for her
Cooing softly
Don't mourn, I can't really believe

In the courtyard pigeons display interest
Picking peacefully amongst themselves
Getting closer
Full bodied and plump
Their throats thick
Oily

Rising without scraping their chairs
Arcing their arms to part the birds
It's time to go
Chapel time

I love you as the sunlight
I know
Grey shoulders bump
Shadows kiss
Quickly
On the doorstep
Forward they skip
God's gift after all.

Evening meal

Jack Sam Joe Bob Royce Benny Mark
So much love in the room
Easy warmth
Invisible and normal
Felt even more later on
Such strength in sharing
Likeminded in some ways
A gentle consensus
To tolerate something
A liberal society made firm
By family
By education and culture
Movies and music
Caulfield tales
Each in their own way carrying a history
Of Europe
Today shaded by the gum tree
Working things out
Their parents would all be proud.

Curly headed cyclist

Curly headed cyclist
Buddhist art historian
Fine man, fine pen
Steeped in grief
Loved beyond the possible
Glimpsed without a god
I cannot tell
Very complex
In his ways
Atop a bicycle

I knew him then
He knows me now
I sought him
He found me

Extended lines on paper
Starting at the same point
Wildly looping ever since
Two butterflies in the light
Excite a vision
The lure of time
As it disappears

Twitching
Beating
Over the leafy greens
Flapping around the lavender
Leaving annoying nibbles
On the fabric of memory
Held in albums
Weighed with perfume

Hailstones
Pelting the garden
Vicious cuts
Wind torn moments
Crispy cold endings
Knees blue and hurt
Desire desires stories
For life it already has

We might see more
As we eat and talk
The choreography of forks
Fielding the pasta on our plates
As we meet
For lunch
To explore how to garden
Art's wisteria
Its whispering purple lanterns
Scented by a spiritual light
His muse will live in him
All his life
This beautiful man
Called Robert Nelson.

Burnt butterfly

Icarus flew
The sun laughed
Icarus kept going
He does it to impress his father
Who watched on with nothing in his eyes

Feathers went black
The sun hit back
Orange dots
And fishy spots
Made it all mad

Scorned, he fell
Dreaming and screaming
His father gently followed him down
And watched his son drown
He dared not look again
At the sun, as it glowered

He dared not look again
For his son
Instead he went home and sadly told his wife
What a fool he had been
This poor father of Icarus.

The magician

I know him
He stands square to you
Looking directly
Without threat
With warmth
Sadness no
Soft joy yes
Switching like a sign
Moving like an Italian
It's a motion
History as an eerie cloud
Lightly borne
Present in colours rich and perilous
A piazza by chance encountered
Charisma in the shadows
Revealed as necessary
Orange flash near lemon-grey
Cherry and black
Deep pools
Olive maybe
As needed
That's Mimmo Cozzolino
With grand design
And art with a line
Spoken and made
Stepping out from his own shade
To give us beauty.

Secrets

Mercury droplets
Running silver
Hues and shines
Slipping and firming
De-forming and bunching
Hunching in the mind

Stop
Waiting
Setting off again
Running like a rabbit

Keep still teddy bear
Anchored by despair
Flying train
In my brain

Snap
Caught in a dream
So clean
They gleam
Reality spilling
Picked up by the artist

There there, I care
Your private world within
A sculptural scene
As a brilliant theme
Michael Doolan.

Natasha Tontey

A village of sound
Different times
Mild screams
Pivot to laughter
We turn and see
Her artwork on display
Sonic and hanging in the air
Natasha

12445
44

In motion without fear
It's a sound piece that refreshes as a stream
Inspired by characters in keyboards
Bouncing discoveries in text

A clever cockroach design
Each dash a chirp
Sweet lamb
And lady with a bonnet
Beautiful

Pan pipes in the patchy Melbourne rain
Weak sunlight breaking through
We return to our car
Past the scenting Pepper trees
Having travelled so far.

Octopus

Stranded and dead on the beach
Twisted lump of fear
Darkening to nothing
Creature of the deep
Not even harmless now.

I toe it with faux concern
Fearing a reflex
Unsure if poison remains
Gauging its reach
When stretched
Attacking and swimming

Almost sexual with its succours
An ancient menace
In watery space
Free of gravity's grace
Buoyant instead
No mind
Just evil
In me.

Before
Before you came ashore,
How many moons ago,
was your fate decided,
did you have a mate?

Of course you did
And a kid
A social hovering in the underworld
Knowing each other
Tentacles relaxed and drooping.

Ivy vibe?
Stretched out sideways and real
A plain tone when dead
Finding food and breeding
Not a philosopher
But living a good life,
eight armed,
or legged,
limbed legend.

Black ink not clouding your home
No longer invisible
Age and size?
Small preferred for the human plate
Tentacles sliced and fried
An unworthy demise
For a monster.

Squids, soft and boneless
We came from the sea
To love it today
Yes when we play
And sometimes when we die
That's where our ashes lie.

I'm on the beach with you
Hopefully the birds will know
What to do
The tide will rise
Lifting you back out to your rest.

Beautiful wharf
for Mother

Walk out
With a friend
Over the water
A straight line done slow
Birds and boats
Sitting and rocking
Knocking
Waves and rippled sand
Pylons driven deep
Mood in the wind
And in the sun
The sea scent different from land.

Gravity-free fun
Some philosophy
Of a quiet kind
May come to your mind
Time to feel the edge
Stop
Pier over
Peer over and down
Look for fish
And things floating around
Find the lapping light.

Reflect
Reflections everywhere
Though you are there
No matter how hard you stare
Instead you turn around
Find your friends
And head back to ground
Trusting the wharf

All that you found
Feet measuring the planks
Bouncing with song
Breezing

As you gambol along
Hands in pockets
Coat open
Not wishing, but knowing,
it will end in peace.

Spell
for Doug Hall AM

To find a cowrie shell
Whether on a beach
Or cold bathroom shelf
Unblinking bulbous eye
Talisman of the deep
Steal it
Before it takes you.

Hold it in your hand
Bring it close to your ear
Hear the waves
From under its tiger skin
Feel its cool
Strange vulva lips
Little curl of a smile
Silent in its prophesy
Committing you to love
The ocean and its depths.

Remember they were once yours
As you see
When you touch
And hold
A cowrie
Play with me
For a while
Freshen my colours
In the water
Stay with me
For a while
Be small as a child
And wonder, once more
That is my spell.

Angels in the playground

When I'm waking
I feel the past
It taps on my foot
Short moments
Walking from a house
Not saying enough
Always moving
Without any apology
Seems to be the message

You can't go back
Look that person in the eye
And start again
Blaming what?
Time itself
Or thoughts in the air
Or behaviours ingrained

Saints
Do they sin?
Is that why people pray
All the time
Because of time
To find an eerie space
A warm column to float on

Mental transparency confounds me
Looking around
With pasts
Moving around on a carousel
Mirrors and music
Red and gold swirls and curls
Stiff horses with mad eyes

Running from my dreams
To crash in the fairground

We walk on
Dark skies and strung lights
Men with cowboy hats
Women calling out
Dusty dogs
Kids with cigarettes
Keep your hand on your money
Not everybody cares
Or wakes as you do
Your gilt flaking off
Those golden dreams

But from reality
We sleep again
Living with hope to live afresh
Only to droop and drowse
Back to the carnival of strange rides
To wake again
Swimming down then up
Breaking out
Odd things trailing through

Too much sleep
Produces too many angels
Singing in chorus
Stirring our souls
To take form as we wake
In endless battle
In the mind's playground
Day and night.

In flower

Free of the leaves I see the tree
Cold limbs with mild moss
Still springy but tempting to test
Cold bed without limbs
I stand near enough to breath heat
I stretch out and feel nothing
Feet planted securely
Feet numb and walking nowhere

It does well to remember the green shape
It is best to forget what you can
Of other times now past
Of other times to come
Bare twigs will easily support new growth
Bare twigs will sadden your gaze
The magnolia will return it's purple and white plume
The magnolia has only a lost scent

Blended in history
Seasons turning
Bricks cold then wet
Now warm and dry
As the house provides cover
As we watched the tree tell the time
Flowers then leaves striking at six then noon
On nature's clock
A serious gong lasting some weeks
One month to an hour is its rate
Two rotations to earth's one
Multiple lives lived as one.

Satan

Invisible evil
Personified he returns in older age
I've just been playing with you
All these years
He says

> Remember your first childhood lie
> Your first theft
> The first lie you were baldly told
> In the cold bitumen schoolyard

> I visited you often
> Made your teeth rot
> Gave you panic
> Allowed you to cry unheard
> Hid inside divine hymns
> In holy places

I'm back to harm you
Maybe to cheat you
To introduce suspicions
Of a world wildly wired
As never before
Except in medieval times
When black ignorance reigned
I revelled in those times!

> Dressed in gold and stiff white
> I preached
> In Latin
> Today I'm in the news
> Appearing mostly everywhere
> Except where it's real

Fear me
Fear me not
The choice is perpetual
Made so to wear you down

For I am a fallen angel
Drifting
Cast aside
By a false god
It seems

Be kind to Satan
Be wary too
The choice is all yours

Look deeper
And you will see
A core of love

Satan
Tattooed in your brain
To scare you
Is a strange being
Born of DNA
To keep you alive
And aware of truly broken people
Who would hurt you
That's my game!

Warship

Warship
Lying there like a lead pencil
Lean and grey
A pointy end with a rocket
The pencil is not mightier
than this sword

HMAS Melbourne
Soon to retire
A farewell to its service
Lying silently at Station Pier
Flag waving goodbye to
mother Williamstown
The shipyard of its birth

I amble along with Alan
Enjoying the sailors' breeze
Our ships have carried us too
He a doctor
Me a curator
Having both served with honour
No shots fired

The warship seems ours
Dedicated and Australian
Million miles cruised
Its rapid missiles and machine guns
Supporting our forward defence

While Alan was in his surgery
I was in my white gallery
In Shepparton decades back
Whilst the Melbourne deployed
Protecting our medicines

and paintings
Which rattled not as
your guns fired
Your sailors drilled to perfection
Thank you, quiet Melbourne.

Must

Get it done
My propulsion
Jet compulsion
Must happen
Beat and focus
Set my jaw
Instant heat
Gone with the logic
I know
And insist
Fight to the end
And more
Damaging anything
Compressed
It burns
Detonated
Fuse flickers and bang.

Re-enactments

I'm repeating some of the
things my mother used to do
Going to the city
Having coffee with my child
Exploring something
a little different
Feeling her footsteps
Warmed by an anticipation

A modest gesture
In return for a smile
The littlest chat
I hear your voice
I loved you in those
urban moments

Away from home
The sorcery of easy commerce
A cappuccino
Forty cents then with
delicious foam
Gog and Magog donging

Ring the Royal Arcade
I must not imagine too much
But it's important
To remember
To respect
And be hopeful of eternity.

JOE PASCOE

Waterlilies

Purples glide

Dry canvas smiles through

Wild-life.

PART 5:
THINGS IN MY POCKET

Lion

Lions padding
Dusty yellow on
distrusted yellow
Quiet big cats
Not much to say
This Sunday afternoon

They are family like
Not tough with
each other
All conflicts aside
Outside the hide

Us tourist are ok
Kids excited
Adult males measuring
themselves
For an unlikely conflict

Slow poetry behind
the glass
They set a careful gait
Like a cloud
moving about
They show us how

The slight throwing
of the limbs
We are caught in
our clothes
Peacocks without wings

They saunter
We walk
They have tails we talk

It's almost over now
It has started to drizzle
on the ochre scene
The lions?
We were not lunch
I think they just
walked away.

Silhouetted by life's riddle

My shadow accused you
I know this now
Brother of mine
I did not mean it so
But you are so bright
Some shapes must form

I mean not to hurt you
Though seasons turn
And leaves rustle and crack
Under all our steps

My voice is silent
Though still heard
In winters night
Cold in the snow

We parted then
Me to art and muses
You to history and its heights
Losing sight of each other

I saw your glow
You found me again in style
Standing in a classical gallery
Landscapes of colour and silken light
Housed in white
Still disturbing your might

Histories pages flapped until torn
And my hand did not touch yours
My love of mystery beckoned
Checking you

Making me hard to find
I left breadcrumbs and golden threads
You had tired of the game
Unable to be equals and plain
Always brocaded we became

O soon it will be late
That time is coming
As the shadows lengthen
To take us in their time

Do not fear
The flames will flicker and flash
Dancing shapes again
Silhouetted by life's riddle
Bob and Joe.

Cowboy

It needed to be
Poetry lay inside me
A lifetime of words
Scrambled then clear
They don't have to rhyme
To be mine

Their shapes echo the days
Fragile forms not based in fact
The words are hard to measure
Syntax papers their cracks
As we gather ourselves in
For more attacks

Left and right they come
A schoolboy ventures
Into the yard
Yelling and whooping
With impatience
Stand back life
Here I come
I come here
Running and jumping
Chasing and following
Over the smooth asphalt

Out the school gate
Onto my bike
To take flight
Curves and crashes
Jeans and genes
Fix them up later

It's good to go back
With variable honesty
To see what actually happened
Back there
Then

Gradually and gradual
Bumped and bruised
Play turned to work
Now back again
In life's long game
Three parts done
Fourth to go
Rounding up these poems
One by one
From the wild rodeo.

Goodnight campfire

Smoky with little bits floating up
Up into the darkness
Flickering away
To converse with the stars
In this sweet cool night

Flames dip
I push a log
A fat twig gathered nearby
In plentiful supply
River burbling
To make tea and clean your teeth
And wash your
Face
At this excellent place

Camped close to a river
Its smooth stones popping in the fire
For a while
Past sundown
As we relax
Into our sleeping bags
Anthony and me
Young scouts we

Kick the ashes
Piss on them
Sizzle and safe
Until morning comes

Overnight dew and a light rain

Soft wind pushing the tent
We were young then
Pretty tough
Could hike all day
Getting mildly lost
On the way

Goodnight campfire.

Droplets

Happen
Smallest droplets
Hitting the mind
Smallest sweet things
Things that happen

Breaking a cloud
A look around
Lifting
Dispelling the mood

Personal efforts
From others too
For you.

Fairies

New poem
Please visit
Come and stay a while
Trick me with a story
Sprinkle your dust,
You fairies dancing in the garden
Hop up onto my nose
Tickle me,
And make me sneeze
Now give me a story, please
Oh no
Come back
You disappearing things
Oh dear
No poem.

Poison

Socrates
I know you
You know me
As you begat me
As I thought of you
You arrived late
I am too old
And you arrived late
But your knock was welcome
On my humble door
Opening it again
And again
Examining the hinges
for falsehoods
Ensuring its alignment
and screws were in place
I had no father
And hence no 'Socrates'
Plato loved and revered you
He organised your voice
Remembering your tones
Laying in the phrases to
both guide and lead
Giving the dialogues a
fascinating dance
They spoke to me in a
modern audio book
As my eyes no longer read
It was in English, but still
There was company and
warmth in the reporting
Jollied by love's cadence
The chicken story

made me laugh
A dying man settling
a minor debt
He remembered his friends
And made them his equals
Sharing to the end
Knowledge needs
company it seems
That's why I like you
And would have
you as a friend.

FRANGIPANI

Old swimming pool

At the swimming pool
Hand over the
exact money
Quick and neat
One with a locker I say
Receive a locker key
And a look that says
Be good

Slippery concrete
underneath
Look for the
locker number
Tin boxes in a
groaning row
All green
Insert the key and
twist left and right
Softly to catch the lock
With a click

Socks in shoes
to keep dry
Money hidden
in the toes
Texan jeans and
green T-shirt
Swop undies
for Speedos
Attach the key with
a large safety pin
Towel over a

JOE PASCOE

boyish shoulder
Or make a turban
Or have a flick fight
To the pool edge
No running

Towel stashed in view
As I was taught to do
Maybe the deep end
Or the high board
Save that for later
Just jump in
with a splash
Arms flapping
like a fish
Swim around so easily

Turn and submerge
Underwater for six
breaststrokes
Popping up away
from the shallow end
Stroke toward the wall
Cling

Too crowded so
push back
Legs kicking too
Across several lanes
Maybe some lap
swimmers
Less the thing then
Tread water mid pool

Spy around
Where's Bob
Over there
All good

Listening to the tranny
Drinking Pepsi
High in the hot stand
3XY Top 40

Warm seats and
a great view
Wet bum prints
Delicious Pepsi
Unbelievable
Cold liquid cola
More special than Coke
With its label and
bottle shape
Shared by us boys
Good burp

Dark dusk and
pool lights on
So calm and buoyant
Duck dive
Touch the bottom
See the underwater sheen
Yellow beams
and blue tiles
Making magic
Wet but not wet
An endless night that
must have ended

A long grassy walk
through Yarra Park
Secure together
To our home above a
shop on Bridge Road
To sleep so well
Shimmering fish
in the moonlight
Mythical slumbers
Smelling of chlorine
Tucked in bed
Head embedded in
the clean pillow
Quickly asleep.

High in the hot stand
3XY Top 40

Warm seats and a great view
Wet bum prints
Delicious Pepsi
Unbelievable
Cold liquid cola
More special than Coke
With its label and bottle shape
Shared by us boys
Good burp

Dark dusk and pool lights on
So calm and buoyant
Duck dive
Touch the bottom
See the underwater sheen
Yellow beams and blue tiles
Making magic
Wet but not wet
An endless night that must have ended

A long grassy walk through Yarra Park
Secure together
To our home above a shop on Bridge Road
To sleep so well
Shimmering fish in the moonlight
Mythical slumbers
Smelling of chlorine
Tucked in bed
Head embedded in the clean pillow
Quickly asleep.

Library foyer

In the library
Walking, walking
computers murmur
Close by, elbows near
Screens tilted
Keeping everybody warm

Is it real
Is it right?
They're learning
And I'm uptight
Still the walking
Walking by

Students pass
Filling every space
Pacing through this foyer
Equal amounts in
And out
University bells chime

It's the old and the new
August University
Selling itself to students
Everywhere
Plugging in here
To super computers
Pulsing data
For sale

A precise form of learning
With digital dings
and dongs

Students inclined
Hand on keyboard
Working hard
Talking sideways to friends
And invisible professors
Concentrated information
Converting to knowledge
In their minds

Walking in
Good steps to take
A place to grow
In the school of life.

Mountain

Piled on over time
Layering a heavy trauma
Covering it with
rocks and moss
Anchoring a
mountain of pain
On a furnace of grief
Pricked by devils forks
If forgotten
Just for a moment

The skies took a
long time to clear
Birds flew and fed
Their calls mostly
unheard in the rain
For it was cold
Despite the despair

Long seasons and
short steps
The rock was hard to climb
And so sad
So little beauty in
the loneliness
Year on year
I slipped

Grazes and rashes
No new songs emerge
Instead the full ache
Perseverance in
the end was all

Just keep going
Always hoping
Though not believing
Hardly hoping
Weak and pecked
by the birds
Fate came

As others died I tried
Looking for a sign
A glint
Napoleonic bursts
of sunlight
A massive storm broke
Causing fear and love
In my thin body
Seen in my eyes
Which were almost blind

Day came
Night as well
The soil needed tilling
As it softened
Purple plants grew
A crop of hard passion fruit
Hanging and dripping tasty
Seeds and pulp
Into which we whored
And the mountain
disappeared.

Wind torn pages

Ink and paper from my hand
Each poem a stone
Of different ages
Thrown or held
Our wind torn pages
Likely stacked so beautifully
By us
That is all I need.

JOE PASCOE

About Joe Pascoe

Joe Pascoe (b.1956) had a long career in the visual arts before publishing his first book of poetry in 2019, *Gum Tree Burning* (Reading Sideways Press). Joe lives in Melbourne with his wife, Lyndel Wischer, and their children, Eve and John.

About Reading Sideways Press

Reading Sideways Press is a Melbourne-based small press founded by Nuraini Juliastuti and Andy Fuller. Reading Sideways Press publishes books and zines on art, sports and literature.

www.ingramcontent.com/pod-product-compliance
Lightning Source LLC
Chambersburg PA
CBHW062111290426
44110CB00023B/2775